Summer 1991

Pam,

On behalf of the Woman's Missionary Union, I want to thank you for sharing your summer and your faith with G.A.'s and Acteens. God has definitely used your gifts of patience, understanding, and caring to lead the girls closer to Him. I appreciate your willingness to share yourself with the campers and staff.

Continue to live in God's love and service. Remember His promises to each of us.

I love you,

Beth Dunn

My Lord
&
My God

CHARLES L. ALLEN

The C. R. Gibson Company,
Norwalk, Connecticut 06856

Foreword

———— ❧ ————

A FRIEND said to Alfred, Lord Tennyson, "My dearest hope is to leave the world better than I found it." "Mine," said Tennyson, "is to have a clearer vision of God."

In youth we dream of great accomplishments—of mountains to climb, of victories to win. As we move on in life, the desire for God grows greater.

Across the years I have had the privilege of being pastor of a church, preaching on radio and television, and to many groups in many places. However, I feel my best ministry has been through my books.

The material in these pages is taken from my own books, which were written over the course of the past thirty years. My prayer is that these pages will help each of us who reads them to have a clearer vision of God.

"IF YE BELIEVE..."

Becoming Acquainted with God

ONE of the deepest laws of life is that we receive that which we expect. Jesus Himself said, *"...believe that ye receive them, and ye shall have them"* (Mark 11:24). But the important question is: How can I believe? Belief must be based on a solid foundation. That foundation is our belief in God. And that is what Job says, *"Acquaint thyself with him, and be at peace."* The better you become acquainted with God, the less tensions you feel and the more peace you possess.

There are many ways to become better acquainted with God. The other day I was up in the mountains. Sitting there in the quiet coolness, my attention became fixed on a great mountain which I could see in the distance.

The peak of the mountain was obscured by a violent thunderstorm. The wind lashed it from every direction, the water poured down upon it in torrents, great bolts of lightning struck it heavy blows. I wondered if even a mountain could withstand such an onslaught. But after awhile the clouds were gone and there stood the mountain glistening in the bright sunlight.

I got to thinking about what that mountain had gone through. There had been many thunderstorms, earthquakes, and fires. It had known cold winters and the heavy burdens of ice and snow. During its lifetime the wars of the world had come and gone; kings had risen and fallen; civilizations had lived and died; but the mountain is still there. Looking at it I felt stronger and more secure.

A verse of Scripture came to mind: *"...the strength of the hills is his also."* Seeing that mountain, I became better acquainted with God. I turned to the Ninety-fifth Psalm, in which that verse is recorded, and I read the entire Psalm. It begins, *"Oh come, let us sing unto the Lord: let us make a joyful noise."* Why can we sing and be joyful? The psalmist tells us it is because of God. *"For the Lord is a great God...the strength of the hills is his ... The sea is his, and He made it..."*; and triumphantly the psalmist declares, *"For he is our God; and we are the people of his pasture...."*

His Strength

One reason people get tense and nervous is because they think they do not have the resources necessary for their lives. We are driven into an attitude of defeat and fear. We shrink back from life in cowardly fashion. But when we know there is a God who truly is God, and when we know He is our God, we feel as confident and relaxed as a child in the presence of its parents.

Looking at that mountain, I thought of another verse of the Bible *"...If ye have faith as a grain of mustard seed, ye shall say unto this mountain, Remove hence to yonder place; and it shall remove; and nothing shall be impossible unto you"* (Matthew 17:20). We become tense and worried when the mountains of life block our paths: debts we cannot pay, problems we cannot solve, obstacles we cannot overcome.

"If ye have faith"—faith in what? In yourself? That is part of the answer. Faith in other people? That, too, is part of it. But mountain—moving faith must begin in one who is bigger than the mountain. And there is One. As Job says, when we become acquainted with Him, we are at peace. Stop concentrating on your weakness and begin thinking of His strength. God isn't worried. His strength is sufficient.

To Be Content

St. Paul said, *"I have learned, in whatsoever state I am, therewith to be content"* (Philippians 4:11).

The word contentment is derived from two Latin words: *con* and *tenio.* It means "to hold together." We use an expression, "I went to pieces." That is an exact expression because it literally happens. I have been writing about inner tension. That is what we feel when, under some strain, we do not hold ourselves together and we develop within ourselves an inner war. We have tension today in the world. What is the reason? Two or more nations are at variance with each other. The world is not unified in its purposes and desires.

When St. Paul said that he was contented, it did not mean he was satisfied with the conditions under which he lived. In fact, he was so dissatisfied that he completely gave himself in changing things. His contentment came as a result of his inner unity and singleness of purpose.

One day he was going his own hotheaded way. He was a big and important man in his own eyes. He could look after himself, he could handle his own affairs. Then suddenly he was struck down to the ground. The Bible says he began to tremble. It may not hurt you to get knocked down. It may not be bad for you to reach the point of trembling. In fact, it will do you good if it causes you to do what Paul did.

A Better Way To Live

It caused him to look up and see God and realize how he had been ignoring God. It caused him to realize there was a better way to live than the way he had been living. It made him become willing to change from his ways to God's ways. So he said, *"Lord, what wilt thou have me do?"* (Acts 9:6). Remember: Paul never learned contentment until first he learned consecration.

David had the same experience. There was a period in his life when he thought he didn't need God, but later he learned differently. After he became really acquainted with God, he said, *"The Lord is my shepherd...surely goodness and mercy shall follow me all the days of my life"* (Psalm 23). Coming to believe in God, automatically we lose our fear of tomorrow. When that happens we are at peace.

What Is Faith?

WHAT is faith? There are many definitions but essentially it means two things: first, to continue to believe in certain truths, no matter what happens. Let me illustrate: A temptation comes to be dishonest. It is easy to think of the advantages to be gained, to say, "This one time won't matter." But one also believes in the principles of honesty and truth. Faith means taking hold of the right principles and being loyal to them.

Faithfulness is standing by what you believe, no matter what happens. One of the grandest statements St. Paul made was this one: *"I have kept the faith."* Life dealt with him harshly but through it all he held to his faith. When one turns aside from what he knows is the highest and best, he is not keeping faith.

Second, the other part of faith is illustrated when man faces up to life and knows that he is unable to get the best of it. He depends on a higher help. For me, faith means three things about God:

(1) *God created this world.* That means that at the very heart of things

are the principles of God. For a time it may seem that evil will triumph but we remember how He said, *"I am Alpha and Omega, the beginning and the ending..."* (Revelation 1:8). God was the beginning, in the end God will win.

(2) *Faith means God cares.* There come times when one feels forgotten and deserted. I wrote a boy who is now located thousands of miles away. He wrote me back, "Your letter made me feel that I have not been forgotten." When one is forgotten, there is little inspiration for living.

(3) *Faith means God is working with us and not just watching us from afar.* This does not mean that everything that happens is His will. Many things happen that hinder His will but He continues to work; and in the end, God's will triumphs.

When Jesus Marveled

HOW does a person get faith? We have the story of a man who had such complete faith that even Christ marveled at it and proclaimed it the greatest faith He had found in all Israel (Luke 7:1-10). We have many instances recorded when Christ was surprised at the unbelief and lack of faith in people, but this is the only time when He found an even greater faith than He expected. The man and his faith are worthy of our study.

He was a centurion, an officer in the Roman army. His beloved servant was so sick he was about to die. This officer heard that Jesus was in his community, so he sent his friends to Him asking that He heal the servant. No doubt Christ was very busy, but He was never too busy to hear and to respond to a call of human need. He is not too busy today to hear those who need and want Him.

As He came near to the man's house, the centurion sent word to Christ asking Him not to go to the trouble actually to come into his house. First, he felt himself unworthy. He said, *"I am not worthy that thou shouldst enter under my roof."* Second, he felt it unnecessary for Christ to come in person. He said, *"Say in a word, and my servant shall be healed."* Those are two basic conditions upon which we receive the power of Christ. Jesus healed the servant because of the faith of the centurion.

A Less Perfect Faith

❧

IN another story, Jesus heals an afflicted boy (Mark 9:1-29). The father said, *"Lord, I believe; help thou mine unbelief."* He was saying he wanted to believe and did, yet his belief was not complete. There was still some doubt in his mind.

The father was not cynical. Even though he had not received the answer to his prayers, he had not turned his back on God. He had not given up and quit trying. He was honest with Christ. He expressed and acted upon the faith he had, but he did not try to hide his doubt. No person believes perfectly. In every human mind there is a mixture of faith and doubt. But the important thing is whether we let ourselves be controlled by the faith we have or by our doubts.

In spite of the father's doubts, but because of his faith, Christ did heal the boy. In Matthew's account of this miracle he records Christ as saying, *"For verily I say unto you, If ye have faith as a grain of mustard seed, ye shall say unto this mountain, Remove hence to yonder place; and it shall remove; and nothing shall be impossible unto you"* (Matt. 17:20). That is, take what faith you have, even if it is as small as a mustard seed, use it and you will find it sufficient for whatever mountain of difficulty there may be in your life.

How God Reveals Himself

THERE are three ways—maybe four—in which God reveals Himself. *First,* in His marvelous creation. *"The heavens declare the glory of God; and the firmament showeth his handiwork"* (Psalm 19:1). That is the first revelation God made of Himself. We stand at the seashore and are moved by the boundless expanse before us. When we remember that He can hold all the seas in *"the hollow of his hand"* (Isaiah 40:12), then we see something of His power. Standing among great mountain peaks, His majesty is impressed upon us. Jesus stood reverently before a wild *"lily of the field"* and saw the glory of God (Matt. 6:28,29). *"Earth's crammed with heaven, and every common bush afire with God,"* sings Mrs. Browning. We look into the heavens and see the infiniteness of God, and at a tiny snowflake and see His perfection. The sunset teaches us of His beauty.

Second, God reveals Himself through people. Through Moses we glimpse God's law; Amos showed us His justice; Hosea His love, and Micah His ethical standards. Someone was kind when we were sick, helped in time of trouble, was friendly when we were lonely. Someone we had wronged forgave in a spirit of love. In all such acts a little of God is revealed unto us. You better understand God because of the love of your mother, the consecrated life of some friend, the heroism of some Joan d'Arc. Corporate worship is so much more rewarding because we learn from each other.

Third, God's supreme revelation of Himself is in Christ. *"He that hath seen me hath seen the Father."*

As you read the four Gospels and see Jesus you begin to realize that you are actually seeing God.

I have no name or explanation for the *fourth* way God reveals Himself. We may call it the *"still, small voice"* or the impress of His spirit on us. But I can testify that there are times, perhaps rare times, when you feel you have received a direct word from Him.

To Know God

MY study has large windows on three sides and through those windows I can see up and down lovely Fairview Road in Atlanta. Surely the trees are no more colorful anywhere and their beautiful profusion of fall color has been food for my soul. It was Charles Kingsley who called beauty *"God's handwriting";* and seeing the beauty of the trees, I do not see how any person in his right mind can fail to believe in God.

❧

The world is quite familiar with the immortal story of the great Tolstoy. He was wealthy, he was honored, he was acclaimed far and wide, but that did not satisfy. He tells how he ran through the sinful thrills of life but they all left him with a gnawing discontent.

One day he was walking in the country. He saw a peasant and observed the look of peace and happiness on the man's face. Tolstoy said to himself, "This peasant has nothing and yet he seems filled with the joy of life." After a period of honest study, he concluded that he was missing God, and so he sought God. One day he found Him and then he knew the answer to that inner hunger and discontent. As a result of his own experience, Tolstoy gave us this great conclusion: *"To know God is to live."*

THE PRAYERFUL HEART

A Receptive Mood

It seems strange that Jesus' disciples would have said, *"Lord, teach us to pray"* (Luke 11:1). These men doubtless had grown up in strictly religious homes. They had gone to church and they had prayed all their lives. A year before if you had asked the disciples, "Do you know how to pray?" they would have been indignant. "Of course, we know how to pray," they would have insisted. "We have prayed regularly every day for years."

They could have quoted you many verses in the Bible in reference to prayer. They could have answered the arguments against prayer and given the reasons for prayer. However, when they saw Jesus pray, they realized they did not know how to pray. They saw how much time

He gave to prayer and what it meant in His own life. They saw Him go into prayer in one mood and come out in another. As a result of His prayers, they saw things become different. To them prayer had been a form but to Christ it was a force. So they said, "Lord, teach us to pray." Their request has been on the lips of many people since that day.

The beginning of prayer is to receive God. That means we must pray in a receptive mood. You get up in the morning thinking of the things you must do that day. Your mind is active and aggressive, and hour by hour during the day you spend your thought, time and effort in your work and activities. Then that night you attend a concert of great music. But to enjoy the concert, you must change your mood. Instead of being aggressively active, at the concert you must become receptive. Likewise, when we pray, we must be receptive. *"Be still, and know that I am God,"* said the psalmist.

What Is Prayer?

———— ❧ ————

WHEN we learn to pray, all of the other relationships with God will come. There are five essential facts that we need to know about prayer. Let me state them briefly:

First: Prayer is "the soul's sincere desire, unuttered or expressed." That is, prayer is part of both our consciousness and our unconsciousness.

Second: Prayer is being connected with power or energy or force, which is both within people and yet completely surrounds people.

Third: Prayer is experiencing fellowship with an everpresent God.

Fourth: Prayer is all of life. It is every thought, every feeling, every act.

Fifth: Prayer is seeking to understand one's own life and one's own self. If through prayer we come to know and experience the God of love, then it becomes truly power in our lives. On the other hand, if we think of God as a God of punishment, retaliation and one to be feared, then prayer develops within us a feeling of insecurity and lack of worth.

The Essence Of Prayer

PRAYER is really the same as the dominant desire of the human soul. We are responsible for our own prayer lives. We cannot put that responsibility on any other person. Through the years I have never known a person to become healed who has continued to blame mother and father, brother or sister, or anyone else—even God—for what has happened to his or her life. True prayer puts the person in his or her own true light. The very essence of prayer therapy is that we are made in the image of God. Get the right image of God and the right self-image will come to you.

The result of true prayer is that instead of lameness, people walk; instead of hating, they love; instead of being critical, they congratulate; instead of being spiteful, they serve; instead of being resentful, they accept.

God hears every prayer. God answers every prayer. Remember, I said *prayer,* and fundamental to prayer is a sense of need that we ourselves cannot meet, and faith that God is both able and willing to meet that need. Sometimes we merely repeat pious words and phrases. I repeat: God hears and answers every *prayer.*

Where God Might Send You

❀

 W HEN you pray you are doing right when you lay before God your plans and desires and ask His help. However, before God really opens the door, He must hear you saying, *"...nevertheless not my will, but thine, be done"* (Luke 22:42). And I must warn you, that is a dangerous prayer to pray.

We think of prayer as being about the safest thing we can do—but it isn't. Do you remember singing the hymn: *"I'll go where you want me to go, dear Lord, O'er mountain, or plain, or sea"*? When we sing those words we usually think of the heroic life of some missionary. But be careful before you promise God you'll go where He wants you to go. He might not send you to Africa. Instead, He might send you to apologize to and to forgive a certain person. Or He might send you to some obscure service in the church. Or He might send you to render an unpleasant service to some other person.

It takes great courage and faith to pray *"nevertheless"*—to relinquish our wills to God's will. But if we do really pray and mean that *"nevertheless,"* then it brings marvelous peace and great power.

❀

Jesus said, *"Ask, and it shall be given you."* That doesn't mean the exact thing you ask will be given. The promise is that something will be given. God may have something much better than you ask for. The faith to pray must include faith in God's love and His plan.

How God Answers Prayer

❀

 H AVE you had an answer to prayer? I asked that question in my newspaper column, but I did not expect the number of replies I got. In fact, it took me about a week to read them all. As I read the many letters I received, I was first impressed by the fact that "God is no respecter of persons."

Some replies came on the letterheads of prominent businessmen, others on the plainest tablet paper, written with pencil. Some of the letters were from people who gave me the impression of being well educated and cultured, others were from people who could express themselves only with great difficulty. Through some of the letters there were revealed qualities of a saintly life which has been lived close to God; others told me of how they had sinned and were ashamed of their lives.

On Equal Ground

But when it comes to prayer, we all stand on equal ground and each has the right of access to the Father. The learned and the unlearned, the rich and the poor, the saint and the sinner, all stand in need before God; and when in prayer they carry that need to God, He answers. Jesus said, *"For every one that asketh receiveth..."* (Matthew 7:8), and when He said *"every one,"* He meant just that.

Also, I was deeply impressed with the complete sincerity of those who wrote me. In belittling prayer, some claim that so-called answers are mere coincidence, that the prayer made no difference; but many, many people believe that prayer is what did make the difference. And it is awfully hard to argue with one who has prayed and to whom the answer has come.

"Take Up Thy Bed..."

A dear lady of eighty-two years wrote that after an operation she was told she could never walk again. "The next morning I told my nurse I was getting up and if I fell I knew the Lord would catch me. My nurse said I mustn't do that but I said, 'Get out of my way,' and I did walk and have been walking now for five years. Praise God from whom all blessings flow." That reminds me of the Lord saying to one, *"Rise, take up thy bed, and walk"* (John 5:8). A lot of people could walk in many ways if they just had the faith and spirit of that lady. She thinks prayer gave her what she needed.

God Works Through People

In response to my request for answers to prayer there came many replies showing how God often works through people. One wrote: "A retired minister's wife who lives near me is very helpful to a little neighbor girl. Her parents are poor and I noticed last Sunday at church that the little girl needed some better clothes."

"I told the minister's wife that I wanted to give her the money to buy the little girl some things. She almost broke into tears and said, 'Before coming today, I prayed that someone would help buy the clothes the little girl needed.' Some other ladies heard the conversation and they also gave and now the little girl has all she needs."

Would you say that God put it into the heart of that woman to notice the child's clothes and to want to give to her? That lady who gave and the one who prayed believe it was prayer that made the difference. I do, too.

When God Says "Wait"

Sometimes God says, "Wait." Maybe He has to wait until we are ready for His answer, and through prayer we do become ready. There are times too when God answers our prayers, not by taking away our troubles, but by giving us the strength to bear them. The purpose of Christ was not to eliminate all the storms of life. He did not come to teach people how to have a good time and to avoid trouble. He came to create character. To His disciples He said, *". . . In the world ye shall have tribulation; but be of good cheer; I have overcome the world"* (John 16:33). And through His grace, we too can overcome our worlds.

꿈

I don't understand prayer any more than I understand electricity. But I do know that man builds a generator that catches out of the air that marvelous power, electricity, and we use that power to do so many things for us. God made electricity and I believe the God who made a power to light our homes did not forget to make a power to light up our lives. The God who made a power to pull our buses did not forget to make a power to help His children along the way of life. Prayer is the means by which we obtain God's power. Lord, teach us to pray!

SHADOWED VALLEYS

The Tides Of Life

RECENTLY I spent some weeks at Sea Island, Georgia, the most beautiful and inspiring place I know of anywhere. The homes, trees and flowers there are as lovely as man working with God can make them.

But I was especially fascinated by the sea. I would go to sleep at night to the melody of the breakers coming in upon the shore. I would eat breakfast each morning on the porch looking out across the vastness of the water. Each day I would walk several miles down the beach. I would swim out into the deep and then ride the waves back in.

As you live by the ocean for a time, there comes a better understanding of life because the two are so much alike. Life itself has a vastness that is beyond the reach of our sight. Just as we are told, *"In his hand are the deep places of the earth...*" also we can say with the psalmist, "*I trusted in thee, O Lord...My times are in thy hand...*" (Psalm 31:14,15). We believe nothing can happen in our lives that God cannot handle. That gives us confidence and faith as we think of tomorrow.

There are many parallels between life and the ocean, but one especially impresses me—the coming and going of the tides. The tides go out and are low, the tides come in and are high. There is no power of earth that can prevent the low and high tides. So it is with an individual life—we experience times of low tide and of high tide and there is no way to stop those tides.

If we realize that we will experience low tides of our spirit, then our moments of depression and discouragement lose much of their terror. Even the true saints, those whose lives have been most completely in the hands of God, knew times when things seemed dark and when the shining of God's eternal light was very dim. There are times when we do not have a sense of the fullness of God's power, or the realization of His presence. Then we say even as Christ said, "*My God, my God, why has thou forsaken me*" (Matthew 27:46).

Many times I have had phone calls from some frantic person saying, "I must see you today. I just cannot go on." But often circumstances would be such that I could not see the person that day. Several days later when I had time, I would telephone and the person would say, "I feel better now. I will be all right." What happened? The tide had come in.

In His Hands

The Bible teaches the principle of "waiting for the tide," again and again. For example, a low-tide experience is a time when we become discouraged. All persons are subject to both elevated and depressed moods. And when discouragement does come, and come it will, remember these words: "*Wait on the Lord: be of good courage, and he shall strengthen thine heart: wait, I say, on the Lord*" (Psalm 27:14). Or these words: "*Why art thou cast down, O my soul? ... hope thou in God...*" (Psalm 42:11). Wait for the tide which God shall bring in.

Sometimes we get nervously overwrought. We want control, calmness and peace but there seems nothing we can do. In such times we need to learn to "wait for the tide." To help in such low-tide times, remember these words from the Bible: *"Rest in the Lord, and wait patiently for him..."* (Psalm 37:7). That verse tells us to be still and rest; but when we are in a nervous, depressed state that is difficult. The psalmist knew that, so he said, *"Rest in the Lord."* Picture in your mind the greatness and goodness of God. Say to yourself, "My times are in His hands." And you gain serenity and quietness. Think of the mighty tides of the ocean and learn to "wait for the tide."

Sometimes the burdens of sorrow are so heavy we cannot bear them. But sorrow is a natural part of the experience of living. In the midst of this low-tide of life, we also need to learn to "wait for the tide." Listen to these words from the Bible: *"For his anger endureth but a moment; in his favour is life: weeping may endure for a night, but joy cometh in the morning"* (Psalm 30:5). Your agony is not permanent. Though a dark night seems to be settling down upon you, the morning will come. So you carry on through your sorrow, knowing it will bring you to the brightness of a new day.

When I was in New York I saw one of the giant ships of the sea coming in. It was beautiful and powerful and proud. But majestic as it was, the great ship had to wait for the tide before it could come in. The captain was anxious to make port. There were passengers on board who were in a hurry to land. But no matter—they must wait for the tide.

And there are times when we are anxious to make some port of victory, to accomplish some task; but also, there are times when we must "wait for the tide." But in the waiting, we are certain the tide will rise, and because of that certainty we have faith and hope.

We enjoy a multitude of blessings which we did not cause. And in the same way we suffer many pains that are not our fault. Sometimes people say to me, "What have I done to deserve this?" and often the answer is "Nothing." Neither have you done anything to deserve many of your blessings. It is all part of belonging to the great human family.

The Answer

SUPPOSE that you could be certain, completely certain, that in spite of what may have happened to you or what your present state may be, in the future the following things will happen to you: Good shall come to you; you will have the financial resources to provide all your needs and more; you will have delight in living; you will accomplish the things you decide on; your prayers will be heard and answered; you will see clearly how to walk the paths of life; and when moments of depression come you will overcome them. If you really were sure those things were in your future, then would you be tense? Of course not.

The Bible promises those things. Let me give the exact words which you will find beginning with Job 22:21 "*...good shall come unto thee... thou shalt be built up...Then shalt thou lay up gold...then shalt thou have thy delight...Thou shalt make thy prayer unto him, and he shall hear thee...Thou shalt also decree a thing, and it shall be established unto thee ...the light shall shine upon thy ways.*"

⊰⊱

Ernie Pyle, the famous war correspondent, wrote a wonderful story of a walk on the beaches of Normandy after that invasion. The sand was strewn with the personal effects of the boys who lay fallen in battle—snapshots, letters, books. By the side of one boy there was a guitar. Near another he saw a Bible half buried in the sand. Ernie Pyle picked it up and walked on. When he had gone half a mile, he turned back and laid it beside the boy where he had found it.

He said, "*I don't know why I picked it up, or why I put it back.*" Maybe he picked it up thinking he would send it to the boy's parents. It would be a comfort to them. Maybe he put it back feeling that since the boy had died with his Bible, it ought to remain with him forever. Whatever the reason, that experience indicates man's feeling that the Bible has the answer for the needs of human life.

Only Human

THE reason we suffer is that we have a capacity to feel. Thank God that we *can* suffer. Suppose you stuck a pin in your hand and felt no pain. That would be a very serious matter. The fact that you can feel pain is good and normal.

Many times we say that death is not a tragedy, but many people who are reading these pages can testify otherwise. As a result, grief is not only human, it is a Christian and an appropriate response.

As a minister, I have many times felt myself in the situation of a little girl who had been sent by her mother on an errand. The little girl was late in returning and her mother asked why. She explained that a playmate of hers had broken a doll. She had stopped to help her. The mother wondered how she could fix the little girl's doll. She asked, "How did you help her?" Her reply is truly wonderful. This little girl said, "I sat down and helped her cry." Time and again in my ministry I have not been able to help the situation. The only thing I could do was sit down with somebody and help them cry.

Tears are not an indication of the lack of faith, nor are they signs of weakness. A biologist has pointed out that lower forms of life do not suffer. The earthworm merely reacts to stimuli. Maybe the earthworm does not need to be able to suffer. Doctor E. Stanley Jones once said, *"If I did not have a cross, I would pray for one."* Suffering develops our souls. It increases our capacity for God. It purifies our faith. At the bottom of the scale of life we see no pain. At the top of the scale of life we see the cross of Christ.

Forgiving Ourselves

GRIEF is one of the most intense of all the emotions. It has the power to create extreme shock. In such a condition no person is able to think clearly. One of the mistakes a person who is in grief-shock makes is to go back and remember some misunderstanding with a loved one, to recall some angry words or criticism, to remember some things that were left undone. What we need to do is to remember that we lived together as imperfect human beings. Unhappy words, impatience, neglect, and the like were all part of the normal give-and-take of living. God forgives. All of us need forgiveness. Most importantly, we need to forgive ourselves. Let us take comfort in these words of the psalmist, *"If thou, Lord, shouldest mark iniquities, O Lord, who shall stand? But there is forgiveness with thee, that thou mayest be feared."* (Psalms 130:3,4).

Not Alone

Sometimes we need to admit that we are not made of iron, that we do have feelings and weaknesses, and that we can be hurt. But, praise God, we also admit that we have strengths and powers and that life can go on. We sometimes think that we just cannot stand this which has happened. But we can stand it, and we *do* stand it by the grace of God. When trouble comes, you may *live* alone, but you are *not* alone.

MOVING OUR MOUNTAINS

We Must Keep Going

THE other day I flew over the Okefenokee Swamp. We were down low and I could see an ugly green film over the water. It looked unclean—a breeding place for health-destroying creatures. At one time the water in that swamp was sweet and pure, coming from clear springs high in the mountains. But in that low place it had stopped, and having stopped, it had stagnated.

This is true also of life. If you stop when you hit low places, your life begins to stagnate. Sometimes tears blind our eyes and we can't see the way ahead, but we must keep going. A physician will explain to you that you use different parts of the brain for different purposes. You use the upper brain cells when you worry and brood. Fear also is in the upper brain cells. The lower brain cells control the muscular activities of your body. Thus, when you engage in activity, it takes the usual strain off the upper brain cells and allows them to function normally.

Love Yourself

DON'T forget to love yourself. That means that you are eager to keep yourself worthy of your own self-respect. An old minister used to pray, "Oh, Lord, give me a high opinion of myself." To love yourself is to recognize that you have a mind which is an instrument of God. It means that you believe your body is literally the temple of the Spirit of God and thus must not be desecrated. To love yourself means that you see yourself as an immortal soul who will live throughout eternity.

In loving ourselves, we are not being selfish. The selfish person is only interested in himself or herself and finds little pleasure in giving and great pleasure in taking. The selfish person looks at the world only from the standpoint of what he or she can get out of it, judging everything in terms of its usefulness to him or her. Selfishness is really the opposite of self-love. In fact, the selfish person is not even capable of loving himself or herself. Somebody once wrote a story in which the main character had no name. That is really the result of selfishness. It leads one to become a nobody.

On the other hand, self-love makes one know that he or she is somebody. You are a person in your own right. To love yourself is to accept yourself as God accepts you. As you discover your own worth, you really begin to discover life.

Close The Gate

MEMORY is both beautiful and glorious but memory can also be tragic. There are some events and thoughts that we need to stop remembering. Again and again I have said to people who have come to me for counseling, "Don't tell me anything you may later regret that you told." There are some topics that just do not need to be discussed. When I was in college I majored in psychology. Even in that day I vigorously disagreed with the idea that we ought not to "repress" anything. Many subjects ought to be left alone. They do not need to be brought up and discussed again. I deplore the constant seeking for hidden reasons and motivating factors as to certain past actions. I am not thinking so much of keeping deeds and thoughts secret, as I am urging to stop thinking about them.

One must learn to live with what cannot be changed. As we look back in our past lives there are some events that are fixed and nothing can be done about them. Why worry about them or why even think about them? Whether we like it or not we are forced to live with our own past. Why not learn to do it gracefully and even happily? Do not let some unhappy memory take away the incentive of the desire to live in the present.

Back through the years each of us has opened and walked through a lot of gates. My suggestion now is that we need to close some gates—and let them stay closed.

You Can Do It!

THERE is a story which begins: *"And he entered again into the synagogue; and there was a man there which had a withered hand."* (Mark 3:1-5). There was a man who was severely handicapped. He could think of a lot of things he wanted to do, but his hand was withered. He could not translate his thoughts into deeds. The hand represents action and his hand was withered.

In fact, to some extent we all are afflicted with this handicap of the withered hand. We have so many good things in mind that we never put into deeds. The other day I was at a funeral and a friend was telling me how long he had known this man who had died. He told me that when he heard his friend was sick he intended to visit him, but he just kept putting it off. And now the man had died and it was too late.

"Stand Forth"

Look into your own mind and see how many good things you have there which you have thought about doing. But as yet you haven't had the right opportunity, or you lack the ability, or you don't have enough training, and haven't had time, or you don't feel like it—all those excuses are just other names for your handicap of a withered hand. You think well but you don't act.

To the man with the withered hand Jesus said, *"Stand forth."* That is, you have drifted long enough. Now let's face up to the situation. There comes a time when we must take command of our thoughts.

To the man whose hand was withered Jesus said, *"Stretch forth thine hand."* Notice the complete confidence of Christ. He had no doubt the man could and would respond. Jesus is saying, "You can do it." Up to now the man had not been able to do it. His own will power was insufficient. But now the will of Christ became his will and he could then do things he couldn't do before.

The Starting Point

⊱⟪⟫⊰

THERE is a story about a traveler who stopped in a small town. He said to one of the natives: *"What is this place noted for?"*

The native replied, *"Mister, this is the starting point for any place in the world. You can start from here and go anywhere you want to."*

That's true of all of us. Wherever we are is the starting place.

Improvisation

GEORGE FREDERICK HANDEL became half-paralyzed and bankrupt. Life for him had become almost an impossible situation. Yet, in the midst of his worst moment came one of his greatest inspirations. He was inspired to produce an oratorio *The Messiah*. Later he told his friends that when he was composing the "Hallelujah Chorus," he could, as it were, hear angels singing and he wrote the music to which he was listening. Today, when we hear the "Hallelujah Chorus," we cannot remain seated. It would be sacrilegious to hear that chorus without standing. What an inspiration that a half-paralyzed, bankrupt man could write it. Such is the God who goes before us.

A great violinist was giving a concert when the A string on his violin broke. Without hesitating he transposed the music and finished the concert on three strings. A lesser violinist might have stopped and moaned about his bad luck. But it takes a great artist to say, "If I cannot play on four strings, I will play on three."

So it is in life. Hardly any person has all he would like to have. We can complain about our bad luck, or we can go ahead and produce melody with what we have.

"I AM WITH YOU"

He Is Our Friend

WE read, *"And the Lord spake unto Moses face to face, as a man speaketh unto his friend..."* (Exodus 33:11). Truly God is a friend, but we need to know God is not the same as an earthly friend or an earthly person. There are persons who seek to think of God within man's limits. We hear the phrase "the man upstairs." That is utterly ridiculous, because there is no "man upstairs." Our God does not have human limitations.

The anthropomorphic approach thinks of a God who is a very old person with a long, flowing robe and a white beard. It is difficult for us to understand how, even if God were a superman, He could know every person on earth. The point is, God is utterly beyond our comprehension. He is so great that He can make a planet or a universe just as easily as He can cause a little violet to grow. God is concerned with each one of His people. As we read the Bible, as we read history, over and over again, we find God dealing with individual persons. Many people say with the great Charles H. Spurgeon, *"I looked at God and He looked at me, and we were one forever."* God is not with us just if we are good or on certain days or in certain periods. God is faithful *all* the time.

Moments With God

Practice the presence of God. There are many ways to do this. For me, the best way is in church. I feel more completely the presence of God in a church service than any other place. The building, the music, the sermon, the prayers all help. Also, in the presence of other people who are worshipping I feel support for my own worship.

I have learned to catch "moments with God" during each day. Henry Drummond, who was a spiritual genius, said, *"Ten minutes spent in the presence of Christ every day, aye, two minutes, will make the whole day different."*

When I drive from my home to my office at the church, I usually come into Ponce de Leon Avenue at Ponce de Leon Place. I always seem to hit a red light there and I do believe it is the slowest light to turn green in town. Then on down the hill at the ball park there is another slow light and then half a block on, still another. Then there is the one at Boulevard. I used to fuss about the delay at those four lights but now I have worked out a devotional period for them.

I have four questions I ask myself and take one at each light. *First,* "What am I most thankful for today?" *Next,* "What have I done during the past twenty-four hours of which I am ashamed?" I limit it to twenty-four hours because no traffic light is red long enough for any longer period. Usually I don't have the time to include everything even for the past day. I confess and ask God's forgiveness. At the *third* light I ask, "What is God's will for my life this one day?" Then at the *last* light I ask, "Whom should I pray for?" Every person can work out for himself moments of spiritual refreshment that make more real the presence of God.

&.

We are in too big a hurry, and we run by far more than we catch up with. The Bible tells us to *"be still, and know that I am God"* (Psalm 46:10). Beauty doesn't shout. Loveliness is quiet. Our finest moods are not clamorous. The familiar appeals of the Divine are always in calm tones, a still, small voice. Here is the New Testament picture of Jesus: *"Behold, I stand at the door, and knock: if any man hear my voice, and open the door, I will come in to him, and will sup with him, and he with me"* (Revelation 3:20). The Divine is not obtrusive. He bursts in no one's life unbidden. He is reserved and courteous.

A Selfless Love

G RACE is the ultimate expression of the love of God—the love that is seeking, selfless, suffering, saving, and supreme. As the shepherd searches for his lamb on the dark mountainside, so is God seeking man, though His love was spit back into His face with the words *"He saved others; himself he cannot save..."* (Matthew 27:42). His measureless love continues to climb new Calvaries, knowing that love through suffering will someday save from sin.

&.

Dr. Henry Sloane Coffin was in China talking to a group of native Christian preachers. He said, *"Tell me what it was about the Christian faith that won you from the other faiths?"* Was it the miracles? No, they had miracles in their own religion. Was it Christ's teaching? No, their own teachers said wonderful things.

Finally one of the elderly men said, *"It was Jesus washing His disciples' feet."*

A Letter From God

SOME time ago someone sent me "a letter from God." I do not know who the human author might have been, but as I read this letter I do believe it really could have been written by God Himself.

When we are in the valley and feel hopeless and helpless, let's remember that we are not dependent on our own efforts and our own strengths.

The letter follows:

> MY DEAR CHILD:
>
> My child, I love you! I shed my own blood for you to make you clean. You are mine now; so believe it is true. You are lovely in my eyes and I created you to be just as you are. Do not criticize yourself or get down for not being perfect in your own eyes. This leads only to frustration. I want you to trust me, one step, one day at a time. Dwell in my power and love. And be free … be yourself!! Don't allow other people to run you. I will guide you, if you let me. Be aware of my presence in everything. I give you patience, love, joy, peace. Look to me for answers. I am your shepherd and will lead you. Follow only me!! Do not ever forget this. Listen and I will tell you my will.
>
> I love you, my child, I love you. Let it flow from you … spill over to all you touch. Be not concerned with yourself …

you are my responsibility. I will change you without you hardly knowing it. You are to love yourself and love others simply because I love you! Take your eyes off yourself! Look to me! I lead, I change, I make, but not when you are trying. I won't fight your efforts. You are mine. Let me have the joy of making you like Christ! Let me love you!! Let me give you joy, peace and kindness. No one else can!

Do you see, my child? You are not your own. You have been bought with blood and now you belong to me. It is really none of your business how I deal with you. Your only comment is to look to me and me only! Never to yourself and never to others. I love you. Do not struggle, but relax in my love. I know what is best and will do it in you. How I want freedom to love you freely! Stop trying to be and let me make you what I want. My will is perfect! My love is sufficient. I will supply all your needs. Look to me, my child.

I LOVE YOU,
YOUR HEAVENLY FATHER